Left to Right

Directions: Trace the gray dashed lines from left to right to match each animal to one of its favorite things.

Pet Store

Directions: Draw a line from each crayon to its matching pets.

Directions: Write the number of pets of each color in the box.

red

yellow

purple

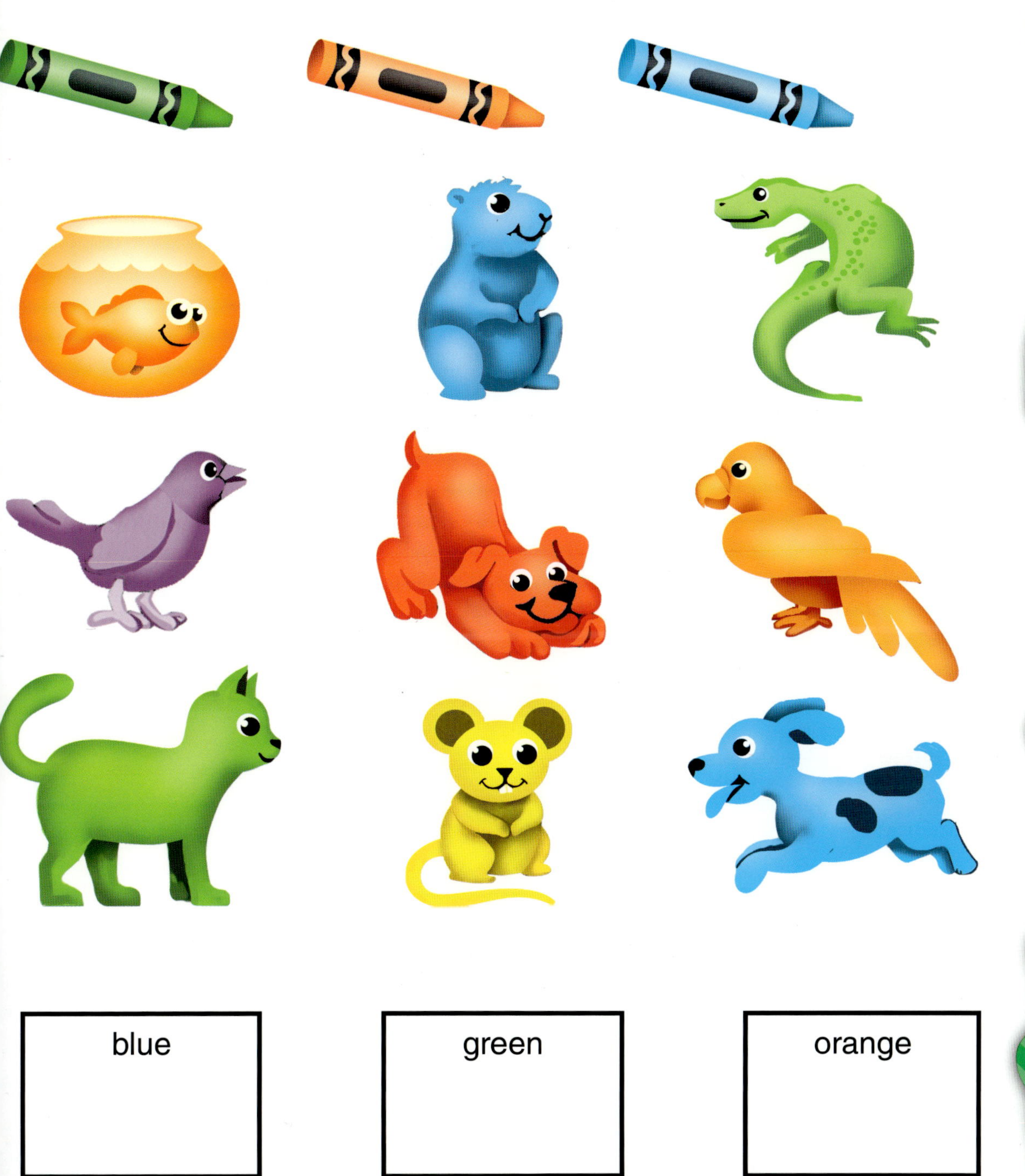

blue
green
orange

Community Helpers

Directions: Look at the pictures and guess what job each person has. Then draw a line to the vehicle each worker drives.

Bow Wow House Hunt

Directions: Look at the different sizes of dogs. Draw a line from each doghouse to a dog that fits.

A Day on the Farm

Directions: Draw a line from each animal to the place where it rests.

Animal Search

Directions: Find and circle the animals hiding among the people.

The Alphabet (A–E)

Directions: Trace the uppercase and lowercase letters. Print each one.

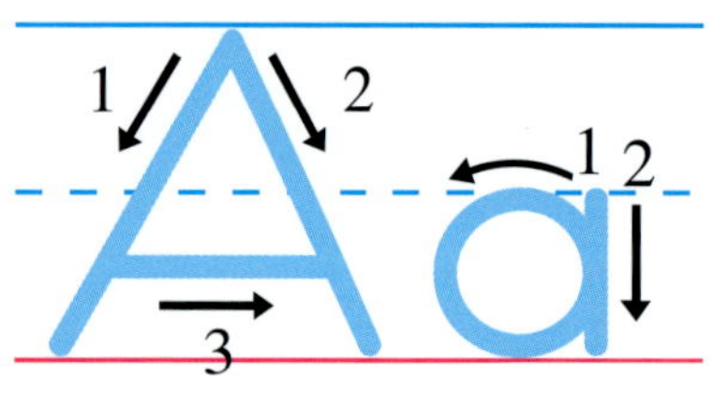 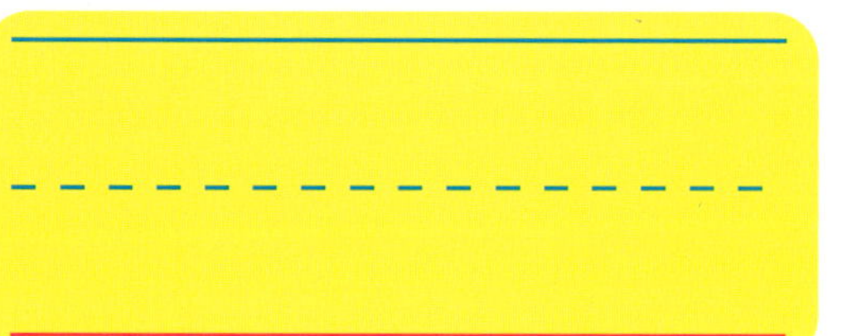 

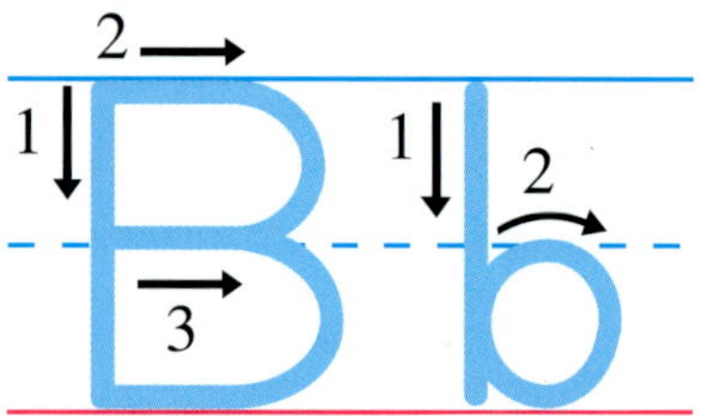 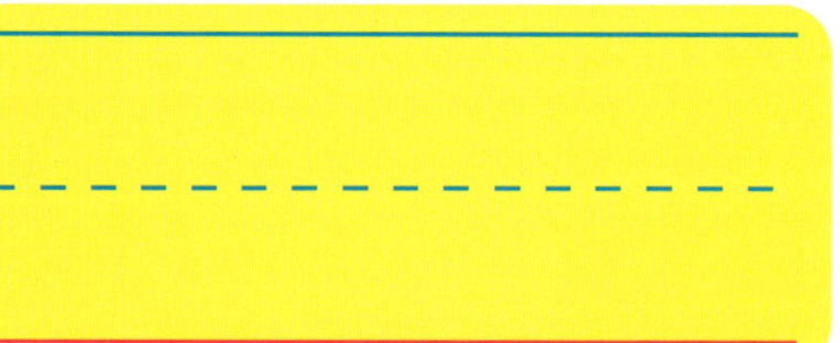 

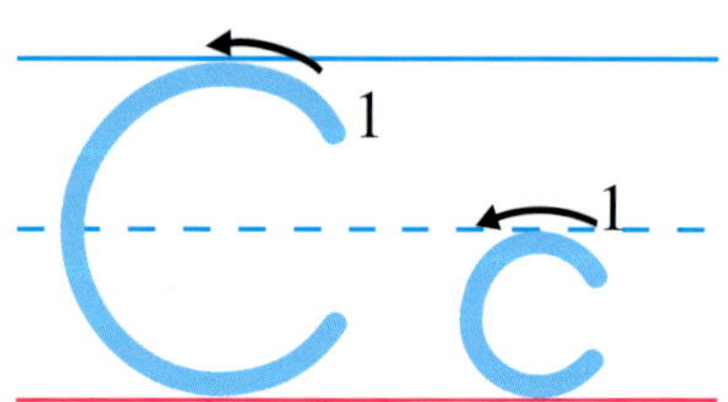  

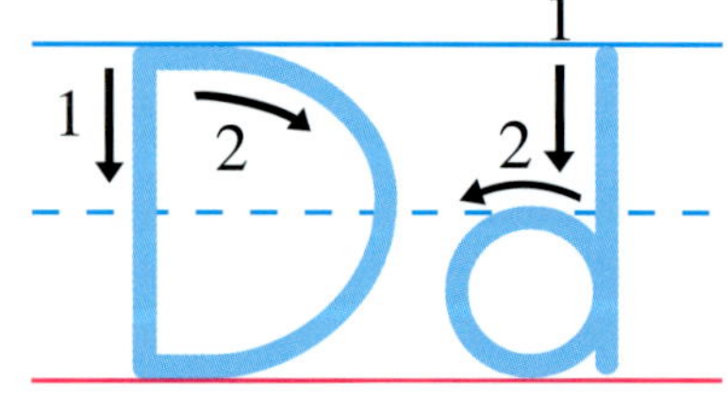  

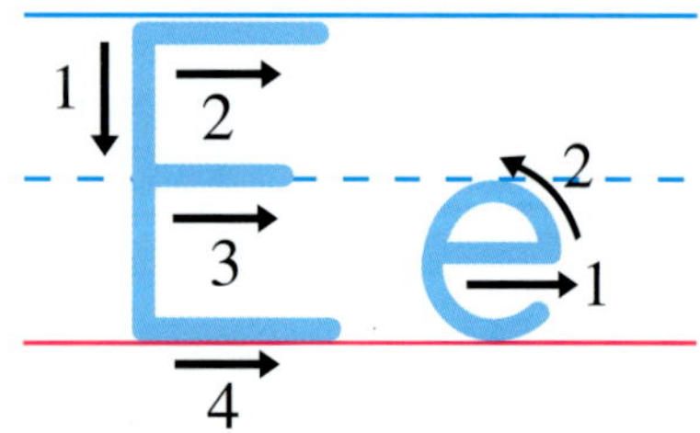  

The Alphabet (F–J)

Directions: Trace the uppercase and lowercase letters. Print each one.

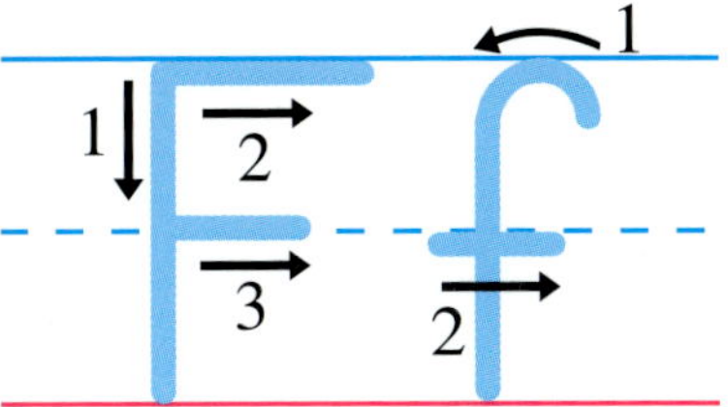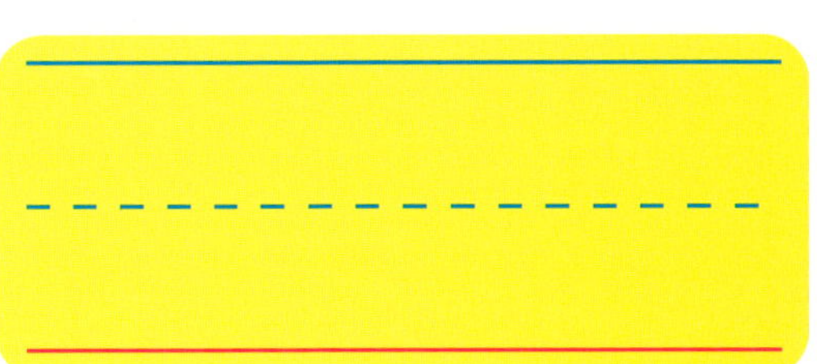

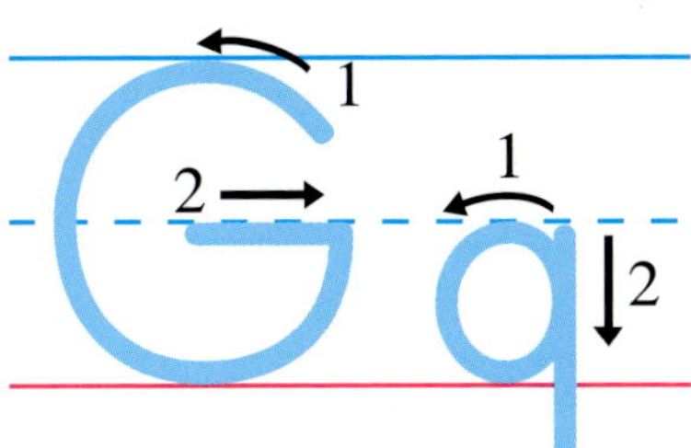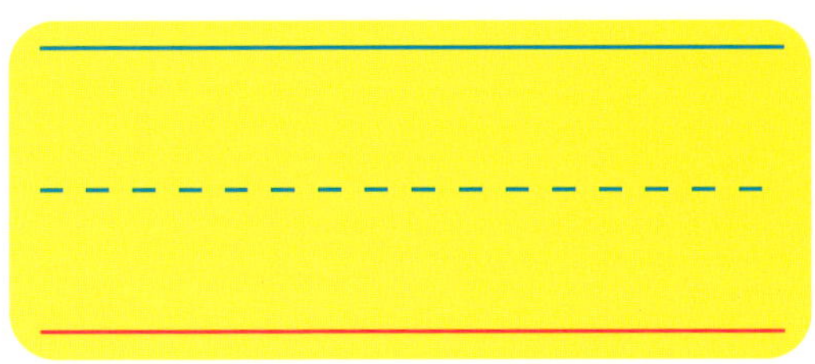

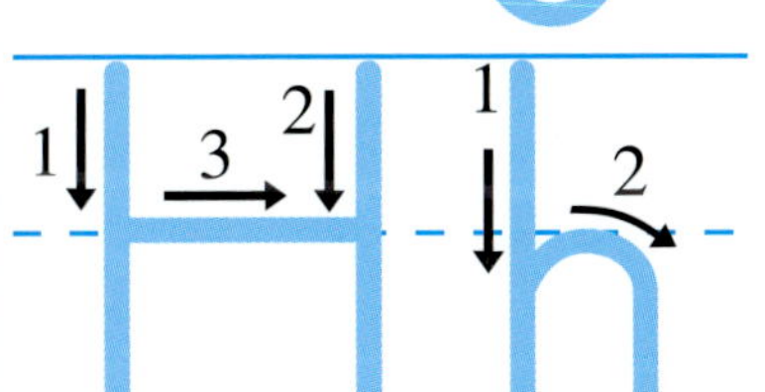

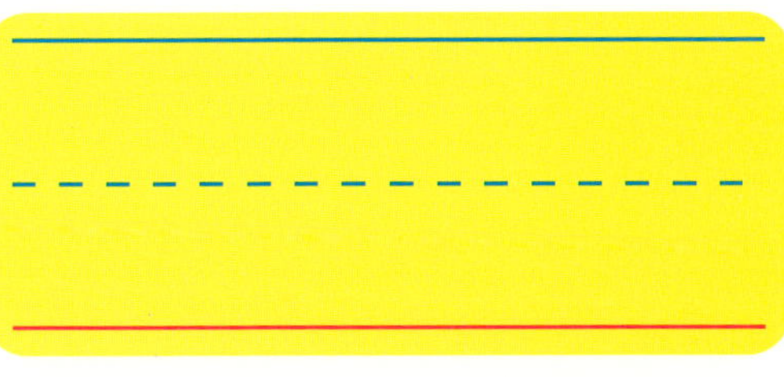

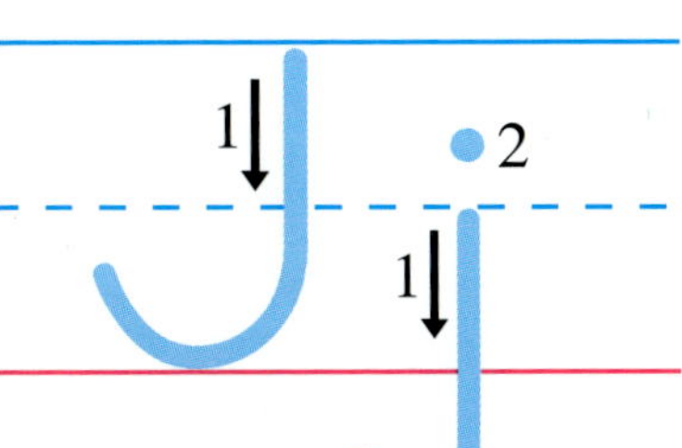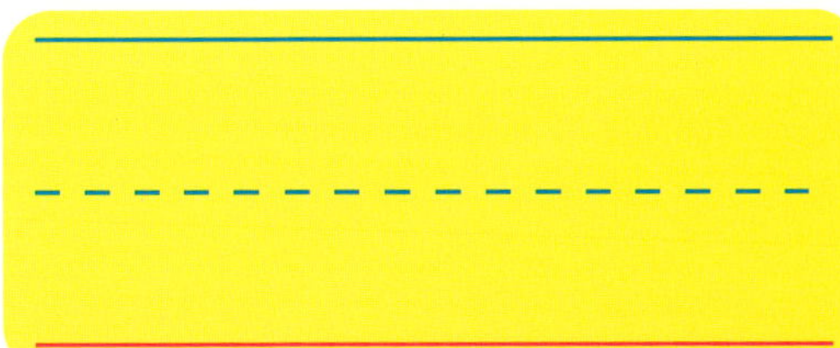

The Alphabet (K–O)

Directions: Trace the uppercase and lowercase letters. Print each one.

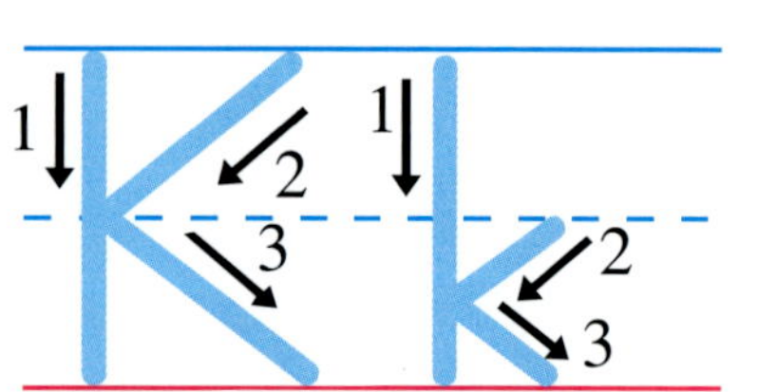 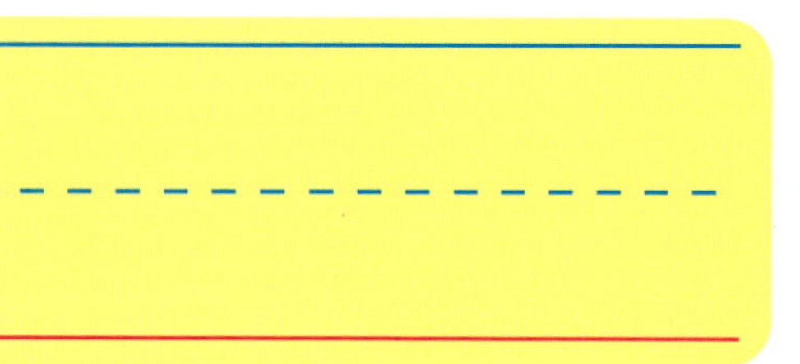 

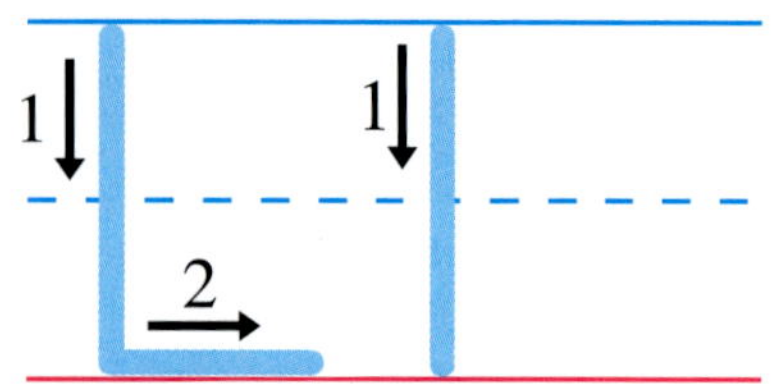 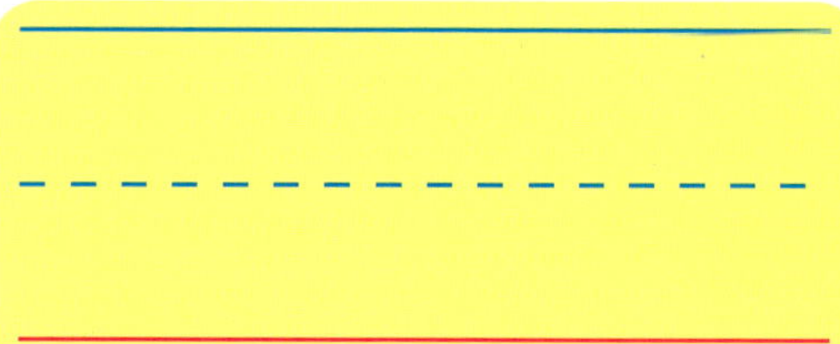 

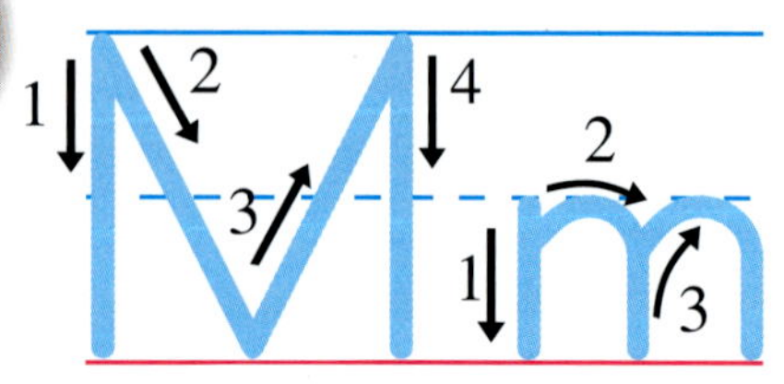 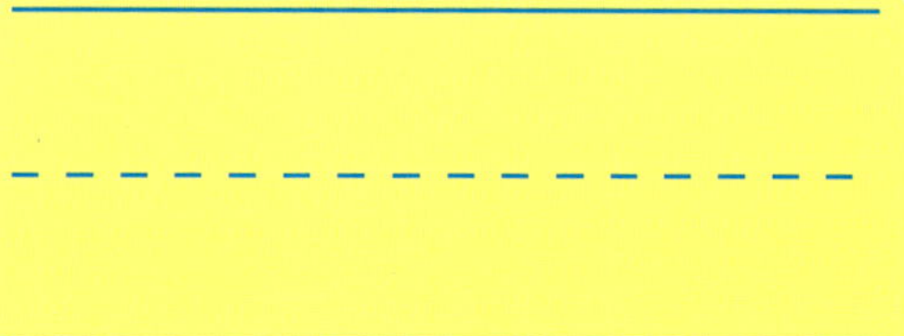 

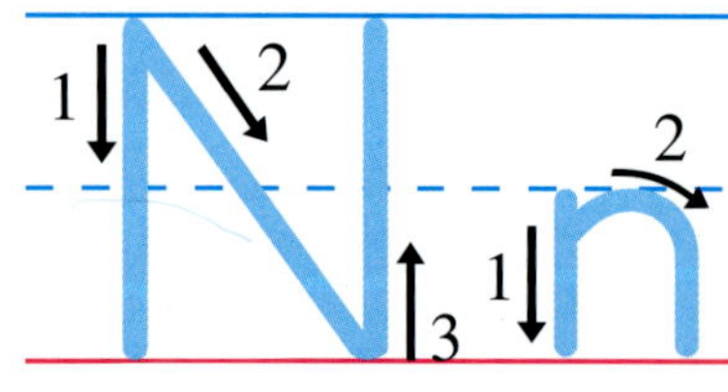 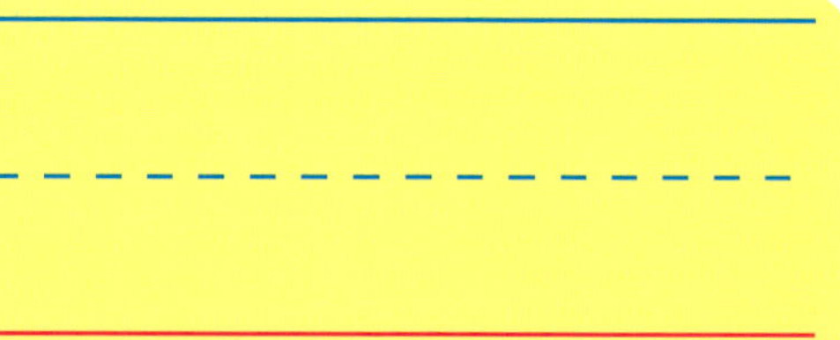 

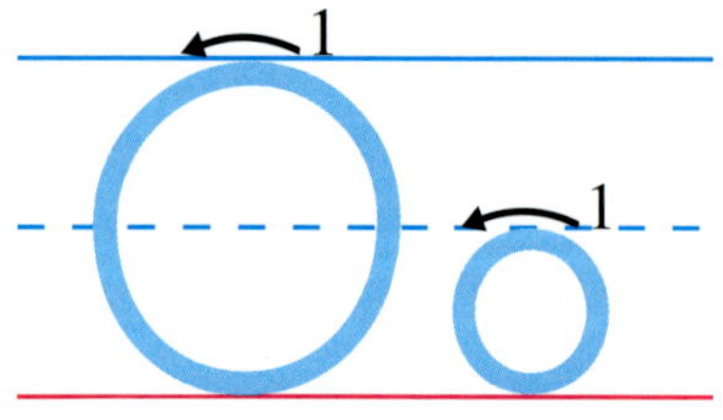  

The Alphabet (P–T)

Directions: Trace the uppercase and lowercase letters. Print each one.

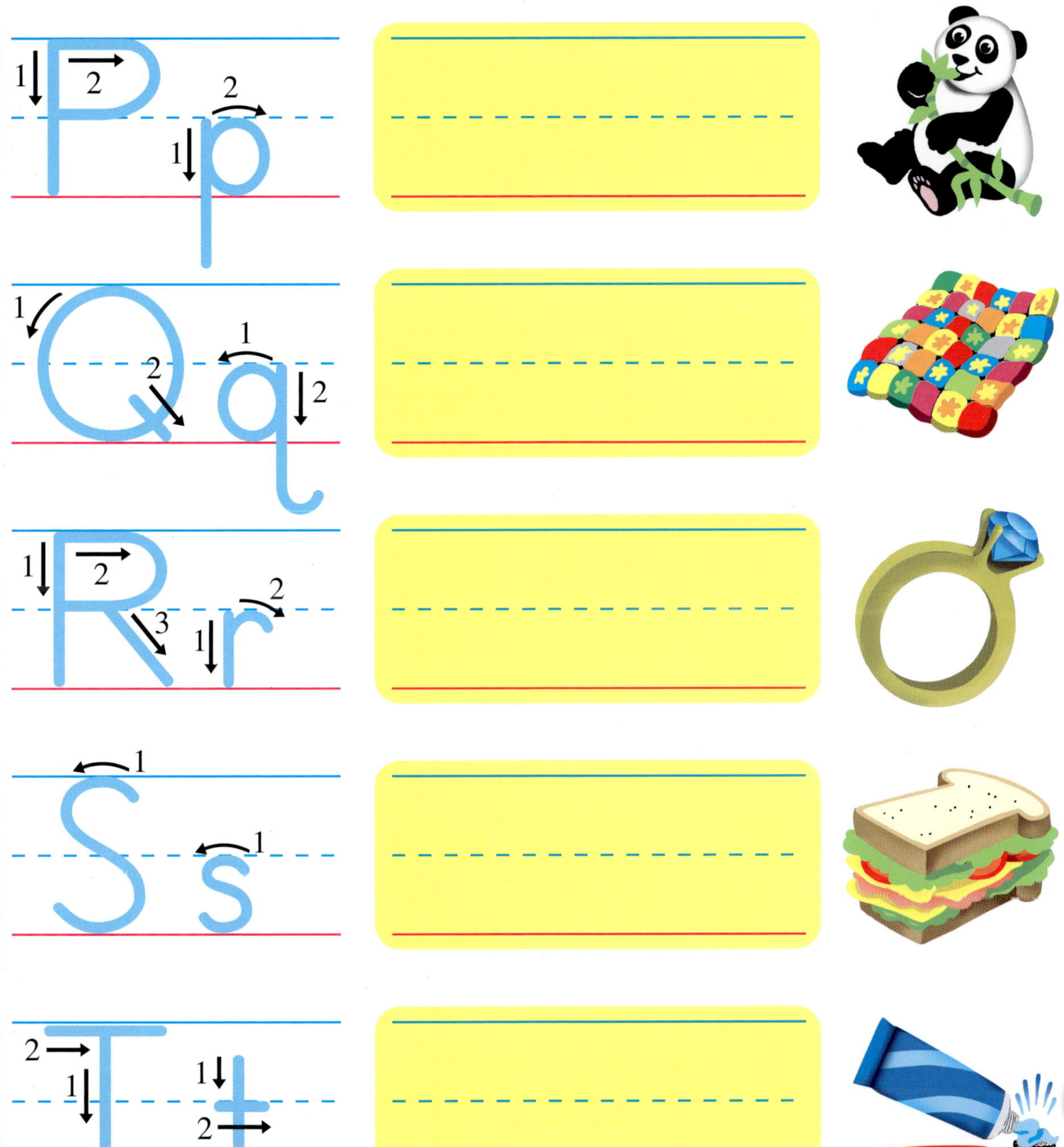

The Alphabet (U–Y)

Directions: Trace the uppercase and lowercase letters. Print each one.

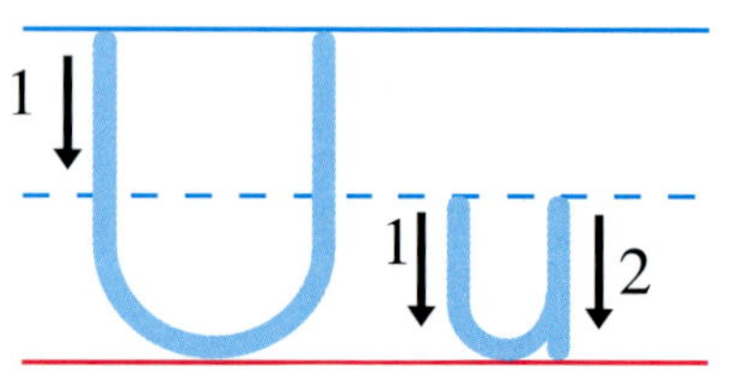 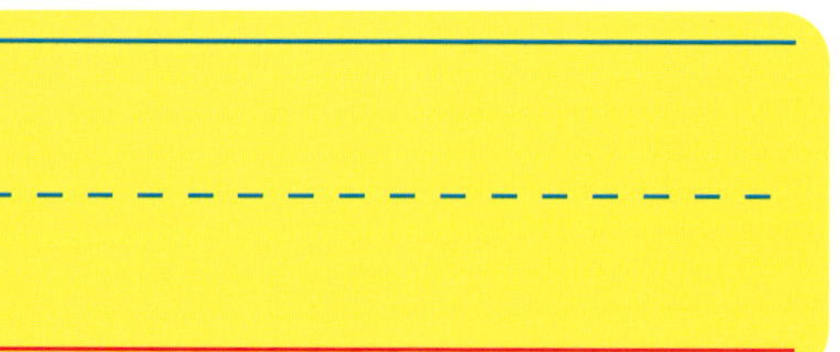 

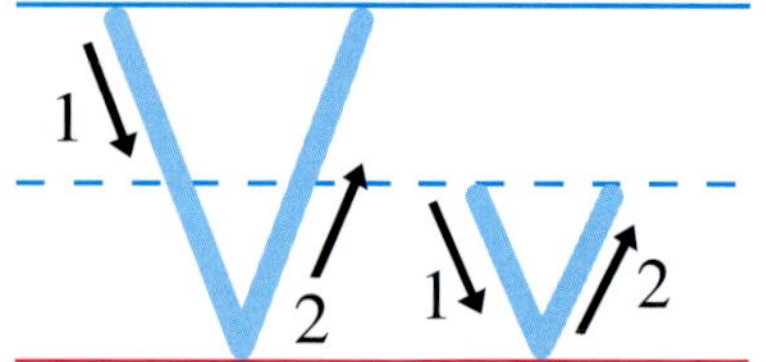  

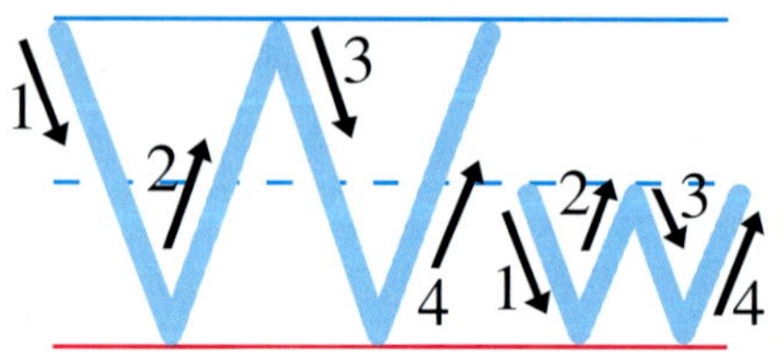 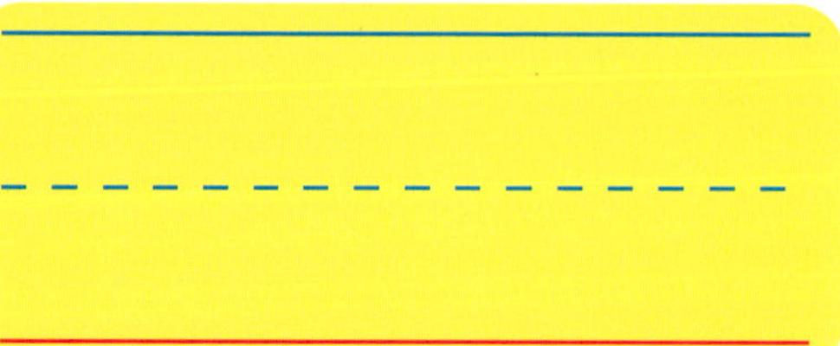 

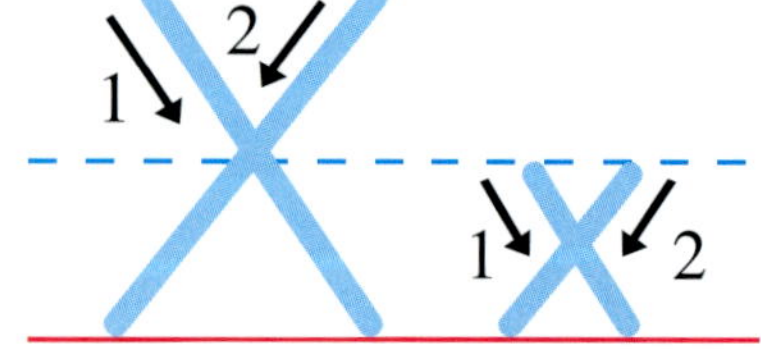  

The Alphabet (Z)

Directions: Trace the uppercase and lowercase letter. Print each one.

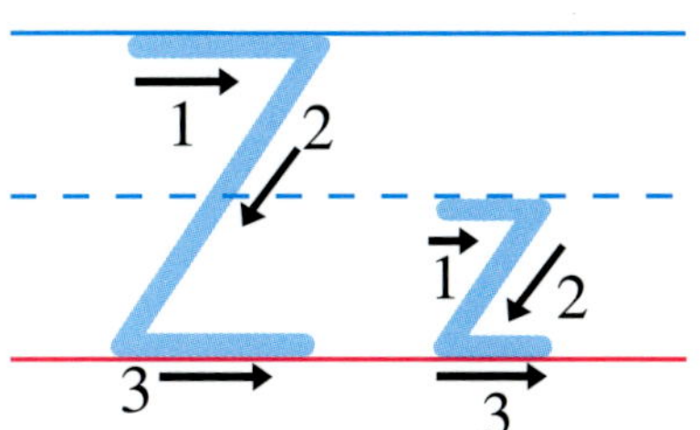 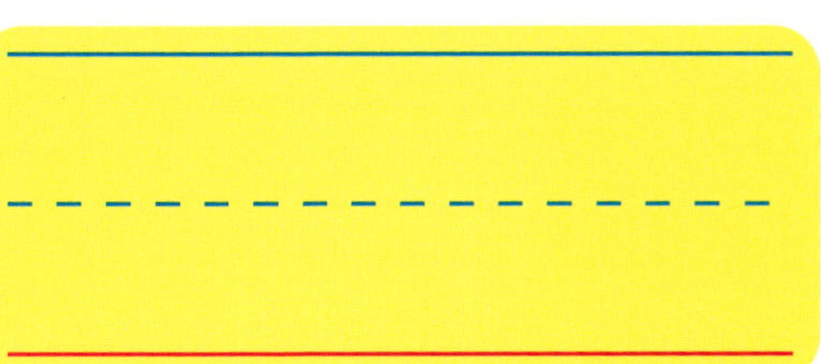 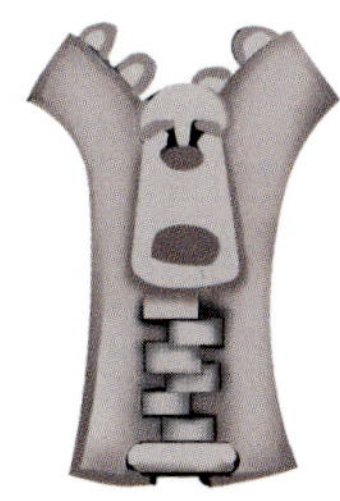

Practice!

Directions: Write your name on the lines below.

Match the Stars

Directions: Draw lines to match the uppercase to lowercase letters.

14

Alphabet Dot-to-Dot

Directions: Connect the dots from A–Z to finish the picture.

Shape Trace

Directions: Name the shapes. Trace each one.

circle
rhombus
square
oval
triangle
rectangle

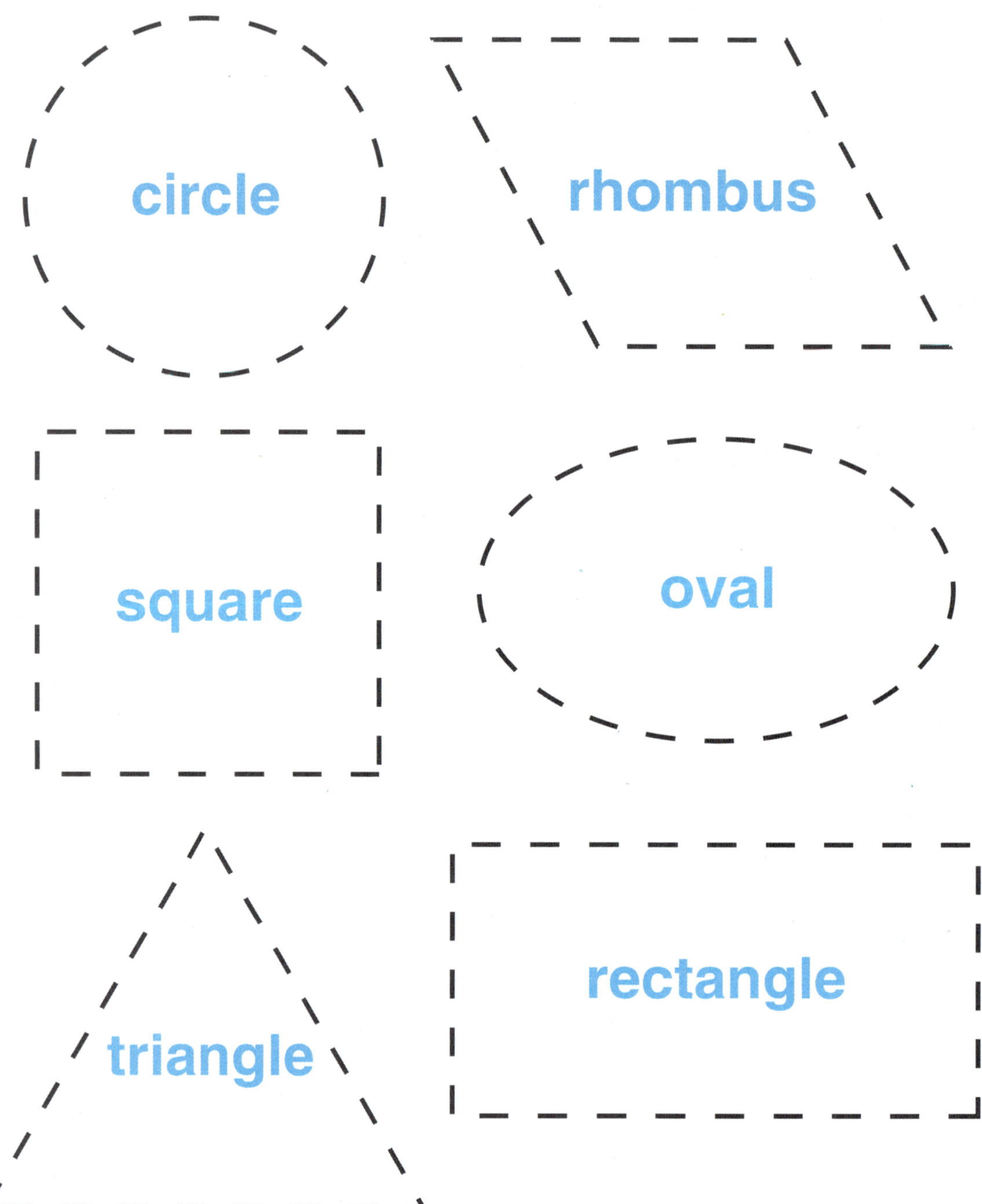

What Is Next?

Directions: Look at each row and draw which shape comes next.

Look at the Pattern

Directions: Circle the picture you think comes next in each row.

One Out

Directions: Look at each group of objects. Put an **X** on the object that does not belong.

Directions: Look at the total number of animals in each section. Trace the number with your finger. Using the arrows to guide you, write the number.

1 Giraffe

2 Seahorses

3 Mice

4 Dolphins

5 Sea Stars

6 Animals on Parade

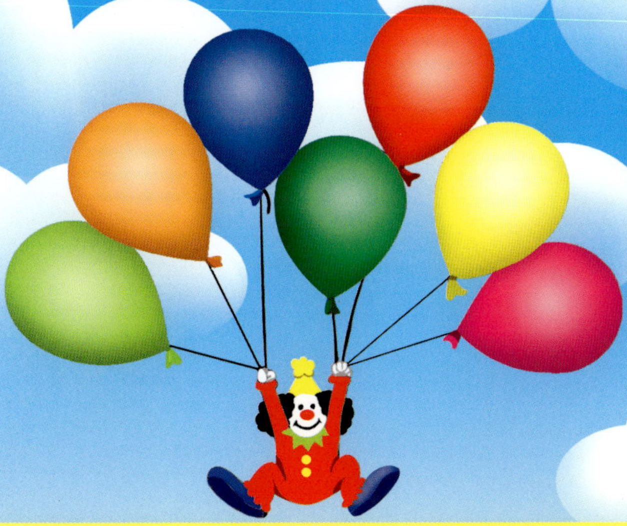

7 Balloons

7 7

8 Octopuses

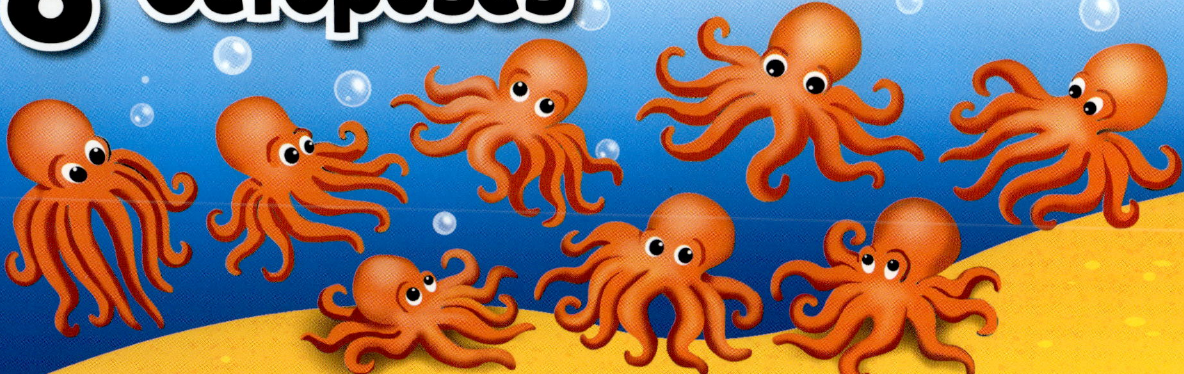

8 8

Directions: Look at the total number of animals in each section. Trace the number with your finger. Using the arrows to guide you, write the number.

9 Snails
10 Frogs

Count the Flowers

Directions: Count the flowers and write the number on the line.

Count the Fruit

Directions: Count the fruit and write the number on the line.

____

____

____

____

____

____

Surprise

Directions: Connect the dots from 1–20 to finish the picture.

Birthday Cake

Directions: Put the four pictures in order. Write a number in each box.

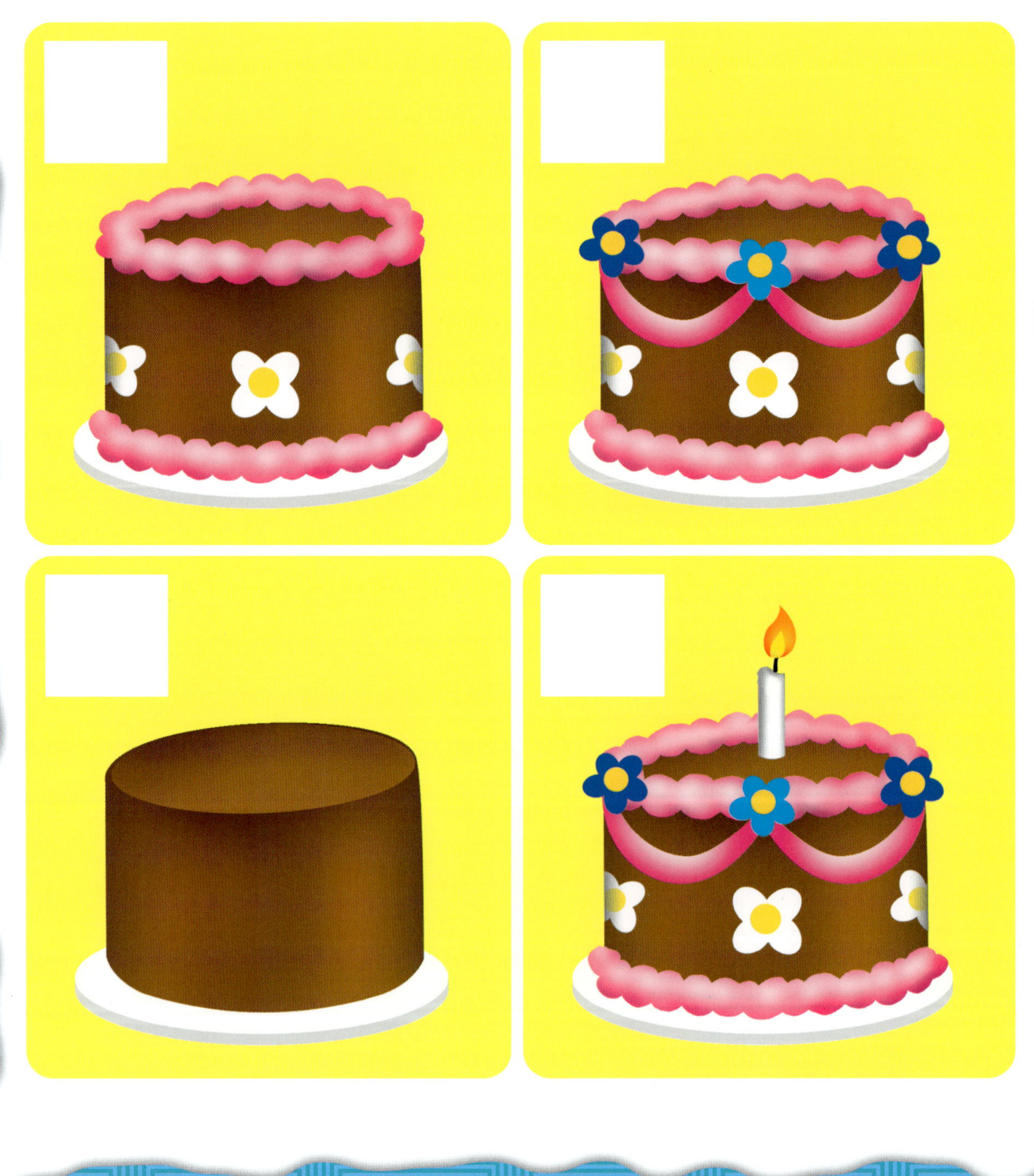

Sequencing Pictures

Directions: Put the pictures in the right order. Write the number on the line in each box.

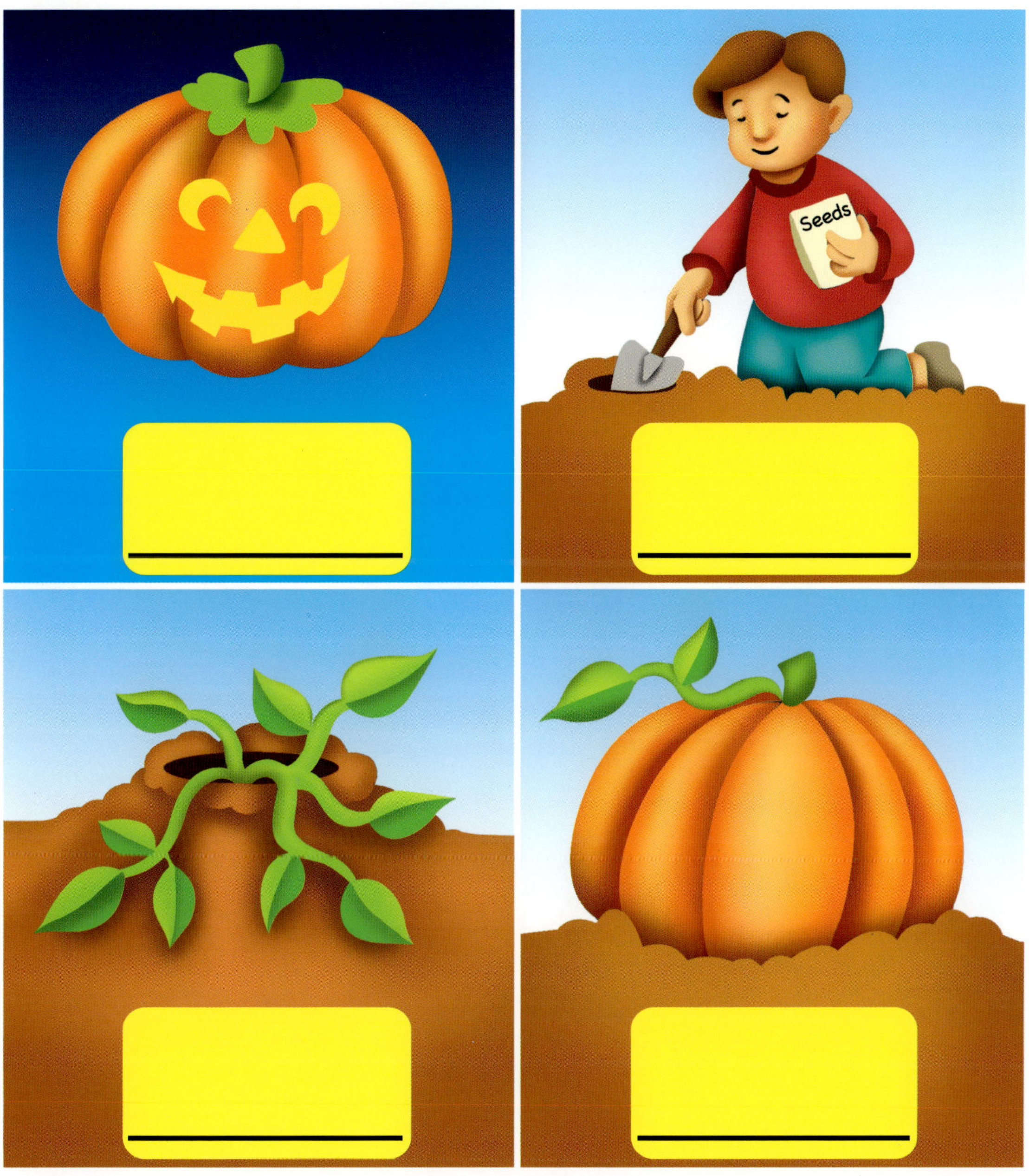

How Many Legs?

Winter Wonderland

Directions: Look at the wintertime scene. Circle each activity that you might see during a snowy, winter day. Talk about your choices.

Blast Off!

Directions: Look at the two pictures. Circle three things that are different in the second picture.